A Guide to Making Rational Environmental Economics Decisions in Five Easy Steps

Robert E. Randall Jr., Ph.D.

Zander® Publications
2351 Sunset Blvd., Suite 170-433
Rocklin, CA 95765

For information address
Zander® Publications,
2351 Sunset Blvd., Suite 170-433
Rocklin, CA 95765

For information about special discounts for bulk purchases,
please contact
Zander® Publications
at contact@zanderpublications.com

Manufactured in the United States of America

ISBN 978-0-9834052-0-7

For my wife, Susan, without whose encouragement and editing, this book would not have been written.

Table of Contents

Introduction

The purpose of this book is to provide simple and straight-forward techniques to get involved with environmentally responsible efforts (also known as the "Green Movement") in an economically sensible and proactive way to comply with government regulations. Generally, organizations need a compelling reason for doing things related to actively improving the condition of the environment. Often the compelling reasons are 1) being forced by the government via regulation or 2) there is money to be made or saved. Regardless of which one is driving your organization to change, this book is designed to provide easy-to-follow guidance as to how to properly evaluate the true cost of doing any activity intended to reduce pollution or improve the environment.

Throughout this book the term *organization* is used in order to simplify the presentation of the material. The following terms can be used interchangeably with *organization*: *industry*, *business*, *company*, *corporation*, *conglomerate*, or *firm*.

The government often mandates less than optimal approaches in dealing with environmental issues and, ultimately, fails to truly protect the environment because it does not take a holistic approach in its analysis. Consider two fairly recent government-mandated environmental approaches. Each one had unintended negative consequences and demonstrated that the government's environmental policy is not infallible.

First, it mandated using methyl tertiary butyl ether (MTBE) as an additive in gasoline to reduce air pollution. However, the unintended consequence was the subsequent carcinogenic contamination of ground water. The government failed to integrate the three main environmental domains—air, water, and land—into its equation.

The second example is more recent and involves the deployment of compact fluorescent light (CFL) bulbs into widespread use. The purpose here is to reduce energy consumption when compared versus incandescent light bulbs. This would be an admirable goal were it not for the harmful consequences—CFLs contain mercury, a highly toxic element. CFLs save energy and last longer than incandescent bulbs, but the quality of light is inferior compared to incandescent bulbs. Further, CFLs can be problematic. Handling waste bulbs, especially broken bulbs, create additional expense because they must be properly managed to avoid the potential for groundwater contamination and personal contact due to mercury exposure.

So, if there is a choice of government intervention versus a proactive approach by the organization to make internal pollution reductions, it is generally less painful to all concerned if the organization decides to act in its own behalf. Companies tend to concentrate more on controlling waste when times are lean, doing their best to maintain profits while the economy is slow. However, they are missing an opportunity to improve their profits and consumers' impression of them even when the economy is growing or strong. Why wouldn't a responsible company pursue this direction naturally?

It is easier for some organizations to identify environmental savings, generally in terms of reduced waste, than for others. Typically, it is easier for large companies with complex operations and processes to capture losses from "low hanging fruit" than for those with simpler systems. For example, a small accounting office with ten employees may not be able to readily identify areas where it can reduce waste. Yet, if they look closely enough, there are a number of places where they can save immediately. Convert all activities to paperless systems—it is an inexpensive and easy approach by reducing paper usage by receiving, storing, and transmitting documents electronically. This simple activity has the additional benefit of not only reducing paper waste but also in other ways as well. Additional benefits to this organization include minimizing file space, making it easier to locate, recover, and copy documents, and searching the documents themselves. Should the organization need to use paper, whether copies or original printout, it is currently relatively simple to recycle toner cartridges at low cost to the user. Companies like Hewlett-Packard provide new toner cartridges in return mailer boxes with preaddressed and prepaid shipment charges. It is as simple as placing the spent toner cartridge back in the box and affixing the label to it. Furthermore, if the company already has daily United Parcel Service (UPS) deliveries or pickups, then there is no need to even leave the office—translating into a time and money saver.

Even in the absence of government intervention via regulation, it will be shown that organizations should pursue green behavior because it makes good economic sense to do so. So long as organizations understand that waste, whether up a stack, down a drain, or in a landfill, equals loss, there can be the potential for resolving concerns that will benefit the environment as well as the organization

Typically where an organization's analysis of environmental benefits and costs fails is to capture the following distinct categories: 1) present mischaracterizations, 2) future opportunities, and 3) true externalities. If it misses, or chooses not to include, those categories, then its assessment of the true benefit or cost of pursuing an activity is incomplete and flawed.

First, present mischaracterizations may occur because the organization is too myopic in its approach to characterize benefits and costs completely. The organization may be missing specific variables (meaning items such as costs for employee or consumer safety, reduced raw material costs, improved relationships with government entities, etc.) when it evaluates whether to pursue an activity or not. By engaging in an activity that reduces air pollution, even if it is compelled to do so by government enforcement, the organization may benefit in other ways that actually reduce the overall cost of compliance. For example, besides the obvious social benefit of reduced air pollution, the organization may see a quantifiable improvement in the health of its own employees as a result. This, in turn, could translate into reduced medical premium costs, reduced sick time, and greater productivity.

Why should organizations voluntarily perform a benefit-cost analysis[1] of its activities? Put quite simply, organizations that do not perform benefit-cost analyses could be literally pumping their profits down the drain. The option either to do nothing or to do something needs some determining factor that will discern if there is an economic incentive. Benefit-cost analysis is that factor. Failure to perform a comprehensive benefit-cost analysis means they are missing key variables such as the benefits of recovering lost material, running more efficiently and safely, lowering clean up costs, reducing enforcement

---

[1] Benefit-cost analysis (BCA) is synonymous with cost-benefit analysis (CBA). Usage in this book favors the term benefit-cost analysis to emphasize the focus on identifying benefits.

actions and associated fines, penalties and notoriety, and improving relationships with government regulatory agencies and the general public. Once an organization learns how to do a comprehensive benefit-cost analysis there is no reason not to expand this to all economic decisions beyond just environmental. Organizations should not require a regulatory hammer to get them to conduct benefit-cost analyses since they should do so naturally because it is good for the profit line. Intelligent managers would use any legitimate opportunity to cut costs and increase benefits without government intervention being the driving force.

Many organizations, especially small ones, (1) do not know how to do a benefit-cost analysis, and (2) those that do are not proficient at performing a comprehensive analysis because they endeavor to control day-to-day production volumes, costs, and quality quotas. That is, they concentrate their effort on producing the most of a given item, at the lowest cost while meeting a minimum quality goal. Little effort tends to be spent on waste. After all, waste is not really all that glamorous. Yet, what is missed here is how much waste feeds back into the overall health of the organization. Cut waste and it translates into reduced raw material, energy, and disposal costs.

Because organizations assume certain environmental costs for doing business, such as those for fees, permits, staff, equipment, and disposal, those are typically the variables included in a basic benefit-cost analysis. Many variables, both costs and benefits, may be overlooked as the organization does its benefit-cost analysis. This mischaracterization of variables may cause the organization to make incorrect decisions as it attempts to make the best selection among several environmental activities it is considering to pursue. This can have a profound impact on the organization's profit margin by misdirecting funds to the wrong area. Furthermore, by helping organizations understand more accurately what is going on they might respond differently, that is, provide organizations with the tools to clearly define the variable that should be included in their environmental analysis of environmental activities. Attention may also be given to intentional omission of key variables that significantly impact the outcome of the net present value calculation and, more specifically, the efficacy of the activity itself. If key variables are omitted from the benefit-cost calculation, then the organization may miss the most appropriate activity.

Second, future opportunities, go a step further than present mischaracterizations. The organization that seeks opportunities beyond the traditional scope will take greater advantage of improving environmental quality. For instance, an organization would view alternatives and opportunities that would drive it to innovate or change with government regulations. If the firm effectively understood costs and benefits it might not only decide more efficiently what activities to undertake, but it would respond differently due to more refined information. The key is not to alter the current benefit-cost calculation methods but, rather, to refine them. This means firms must incorporate variables that may have been overlooked or underestimated in the past. Then, they need to incorporate the results of this refined approach in their strategic planning. The use of such methodology should lead to more effective decision making with attendant economic benefits for the organizations.

Organizations need to look beyond the here and now as they assess benefits and costs. They need to look at the whole life of the activities to determine if it is efficacious to pursue it. So, in effect, there is a time component of the analysis. Additionally, there is a directional component, too. Take into account that when attempting to influence a corporate strategy, horizontal and vertical components of the organization come into play. An example of this is the organization where it needs to control air emissions of volatile organic compounds. If the organization has more than one facility that needs to do so, then there is an opportunity to reapply engineering and design costs to reduce the overall cost had the organization only one location. Additionally, economies of scale can come into play if an organization buys more than one piece of pollution control technology. Generally, large organizations enjoy benefit of the economies of scale to a greater extent than smaller organizations. They get more bang from their buck. The organization reduces its total costs by deploying the same technology across its organization. There may also be an opportunity if they developed a unique pollution control technology or process to license, market, sell, or trade that technology at a substantial profit for the organization. The basic message is to integrate the entire organization so that its corporate strategy includes environmental activities as a key part of doing business while employing and deploying the most economically sound approach for doing so.

Third, true externalities are produced by an economic unit that impacts society's resources by where the impact is not fully felt by the producer. In some cases, activities by the organization that negatively impact the environment cannot be controlled by reducing the

7

organization's profits in the short or long run. In most of these cases the firm would have no incentive to do anything to reduce pollution on its own. The exception to this would be if the organization could benefit in the marketplace from a more pro-environmental image.

More and more organizations are promoting a "green" marketing strategy as a positive way of representing the firm. It presents an image that the organization has virtue (i.e., it cares for the environment and society in general). It could be argued that firms are anything but altruistic as their purpose in business is to make money. Consequently, the "green" marketing strategy is just that, a strategy to earn profits for the organization. Certainly, there are benefits for society, but would the organization pursue them if it were not for economic gain? Such a firm would not stay in business long. Thus, it must be kept in mind that it is the benefits from an enhanced corporate image that causes the organization to make its decision to actively invest in "green" pursuits.

It should be clearly stated that a value judgment against government regulations that control the impact on the environment by organizations is not being made here. Quite frankly, one begs to ask the question had it not been for government regulation would organizations have voluntarily taken steps to control their discharges or emissions. Whole new opportunities were probably initiated as a result of environmental regulations. Once being forced to reduce environmental impacts, some organizations started to see some additional benefits, so long as they were looking for them. The organization that cleans up to a point required by law may have learned some techniques that allow it to clean up even more and obtain continued regards. However, by being environmentally conscientious, the organization may also convey to

8

society that it is contributing to the quality of the regional environment. Benefits it may reap from its investment include enticing workers and managers for whom environmental quality is key, or who take pride in and want to work for a firm that is a responsible environmental neighbor. If these workers are more productive than the average worker, then the organization benefits from their efforts. These variables are difficult to include in the benefit-cost calculation because they are so difficult to quantify, mainly because most organizations have not learned how to estimate intangible costs yet. Where they can be particularly important is at the point where the benefits may equal the costs, or slightly less. By taking into account the social aspects, the organization may have its decision influenced to pursue an activity it might not have otherwise pursued.

An example of this is an organization considering a pro-environment change, but for which the benefit-cost analysis suggest that it is not worth anything to the organization directly to do it. However, the change benefits society. The organization may decide that later positive yields for its pro-environment image make the change worth-while, even though in the short-run it loses money.

Certainly few, if any, organizations would consider the cost of true externalities because they will not benefit directly from reducing these costs unless future regulation force them to internalize them or they are able to increase demand for their products based on their green image.

Let's be clear. There are times, based on an economic and social evaluation, when activities should not be done because there is no clear or compelling reason to do so. The primary purpose for doing this assessment is to make a rational, economics-based, decision whether to do it or not do it.

The Green Philosophy

Organizations, other than those acting as social entities like non-profits, are generally not altruistic. They are in business to make money for themselves and their investors. Otherwise, there would be no compelling reason for them to be in business. They expand based on need due to increased demand for their products or services or a competitive edge, which translates into higher profits. This, in turn, generally increases their impact on the environment because they tend to generate more waste by discharging more wastewater, increasing their air emissions, and sending more trash to the landfill.

With more emphasis on the green movement, organizations are trying to live up to the public's expectations of environmentally appropriate operation. There is an active movement to grant products green status if they are packaged with recycled or easily recyclable materials.

In fact, there is an opportunity to realize greater profitability due to this distinct advantage over competitors. One way that the green approach works is my ensuring consistent quality of the products produced. This prevents rework or disposal of off-quality product.

By decreasing, or downsizing, packaging contents, including the thickness of wrapping, businesses can have a significant impact on the total cost of the product and amount of material disposed.

This brings us to sustainable development, which is an important part of the green philosophy. Sustainable development promotes use of resources in order to provide for today's needs, but not at a cost to future generations. This, in part, means that we use renewable resources at a rate to they are naturally replaced (e.g., forestry products and fisheries) without depleting supplies, and non renewable resources (e.g., oil, coal, gas, and minerals) used intelligently so they are not wasted or misused. This does not apply only to raw materials, but includes the effects of disposal of wastes on the environment and how they might impact future generations.

Another way to implement the green philosophy is to incorporate green chemistry where possible, particularly in chemical manufacturing operations or any situation employing blending, mixing, reacting, etc. There are a number of approaches to deploy this strategy. This could mean a reformulation of the chemistry, substitution of a hazardous chemical with non-hazardous or less hazardous chemical, or improving the reaction completion.

By performing a life cycle analysis (LCA) it is possible to determine the impact in every step of a chemical's life. This begins from the time it is mined or created and proceeds throughout its handling, processing, reaction, reuse and recycle, and ultimate disposal. It even extends beyond disposal because its effects do not end there. Ultimately, this is where concern about the chemical escalates with possible impact upon the environment and society via groundwater, air, and land contamination.

The Benefit-Cost Model

Historically, organizations have performed benefit-cost analyses using a fairly simple and archaic approach. This is what will be referred to as a Traditional Benefit-Cost Model. Figure 1 presents such a generic model for demonstration purposes. It illustrates how organizations have typically used benefit-cost analysis in a very limited fashion with equally limited characterization of variables and their impact on the benefit-cost calculus. This illustration represents the way in which an organization interprets regulatory impact upon the organization and how the cost to comply with regulations far outweighed the benefits if, in fact, there were any benefits. Many organizations continue to take this myopic view; otherwise, we would see fewer emissions, discharges, and other related environmental issues. Although there are benefits in addition to pre-consumer recycling, few organizations pursued much more than this. It has only been in recent years that organizations are looking at environmental costs from a more holistic viewpoint, like post-consumer recycling, productivity enhancements, and personnel safety. This model misses many attributes or variables necessary to make an informed decision.

COSTS

Permits, Fees,
Fines

BENEFITS

COSTS

Compliance Costs
(Staff, Paperwork,
Legal)

Regulatory Impacts

Pre-consumer
Recycling

COSTS

Pollution Control
Technology Costs

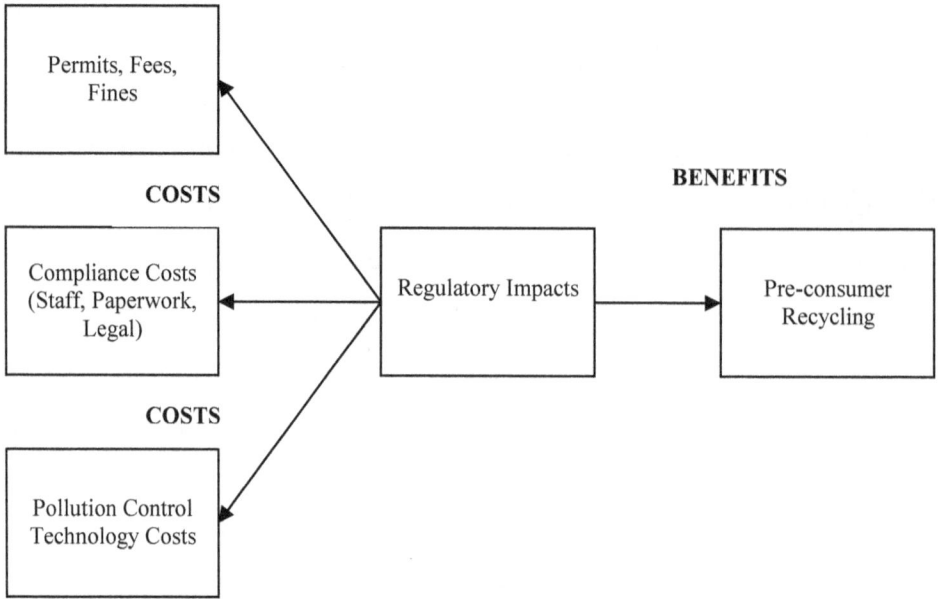

Figure 1. Traditional Benefit-Cost Model.

What is proposed here is a more comprehensive characterization of variables or attributes used in the benefit-cost calculation, that is, a Refined Benefit-Cost Model. This includes both tangible and intangible costs and benefits, and direct and indirect costs and benefits. Figure 2 is a generic representation of the Refined Benefit-Cost Model (Randall, 1999). Generally, organizations tend to think in terms of tangible and direct costs. One reason this happens is because it is easy to apply hard dollars when the organization's strategic initiative needs to be defined and modified. It is also much easier to justify such costs and benefits to investors. Although they may be difficult to accurately quantify, there may be many intangible variables that provide substantial benefit to the organization. Even if the leaders of an organization make a conservative estimate of their value compared to associated costs, they could conceivably choose to include them in the total cost calculus. This could

14

be viewed as an opportunity cost; that is, a cost that has a previously unanticipated benefit.

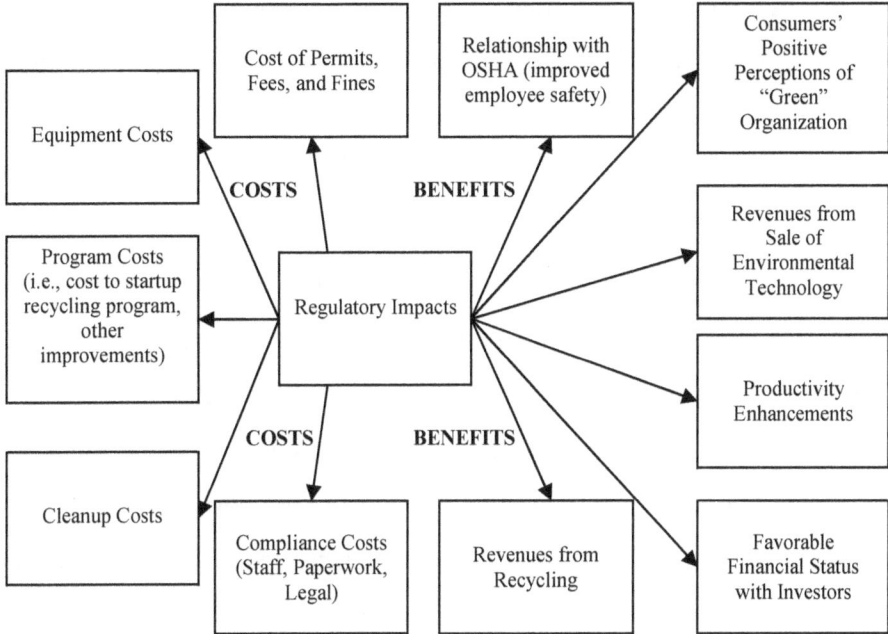

Figure 2. Refined Benefit-Cost Model.

The number of variables represented in the model is dependent upon how refined the organization needs to make the model and how well it can separate individual variables. It is somewhat dependent upon how much importance the particular organization places on the given variable. The model can also be simplified in cases where certain variables carry little relative weight in the overall calculation. Remember, the model needs to be customized to each organization's situation.

The importance of this exercise is to determine if the firm should act. To make an intelligent and informed decision, the organization needs to accurately identify each variable for each function of the algorithm. Only then can the organization properly evaluate the appropriateness of doing the environmental, or for that matter, any activity. It should be noted that some variables should be relatively easy to quantify, especially costs such as compliance, cleanup, equipment, and fees. By the same token, some benefits are fairly easy to measure. These include revenues from the sale of environmental control technology, recycling revenues, or the added value of employee safety.

A critical aspect of the Refined Benefit-Cost Model is that as the organization reduces its environmental liabilities, it converts costs into benefits. If the organization does not have to pay to litigate cases of non-compliance, then we have what can be called cost avoidance or, more correctly, a benefit. The goal here is to reduce the variables on the cost side of the equation and move them to the benefit side. This can include both tangible and intangible variables. Variables, such as positive consumer perception or aesthetic benefits (actions that improve the appearance, perceived or real, of the organization to the regulatory community) tend to be much more difficult to quantify. There are, nonetheless, widely accepted methods to determine such intangibles.

Historically, society has suffered as a result of external environmental costs. We are all paying for Superfund cleanup where no potentially responsible party exists. We are all paying via our taxes for enforcement action, and we are all paying via increased prices for organizational environmental mistakes from the past. Therefore, the way an organization internalizes those costs is important in the overall cost calculus. But, that is only one side of the coin. If organizations are expected to internalize environmental costs, then, perhaps there are methods to offset those costs with previously unaccounted for benefits.

Tangible and Intangible Costs and Benefits

Organizations tend to focus solely on tangible, or direct, costs, as opposed to intangible, or indirect, costs. Direct costs are those than can generally be itemized as a budgetary line item. Those costs include items such as employee salaries and benefits, capital costs, equipment repair costs, and operating expenses like supplies, raw materials, energy costs, transportation costs, and marketing costs. These are fairly easy to identify, estimate, and quantify. By looking at past spending history the organization can predict their future spending, building into estimate a percentage to account for inflation or other external influences.

It is when intangibles are brought up that the discussion becomes more esoteric. Nonetheless, those intangibles could, in fact, have a greater impact on the wellbeing of the organization than the intangibles. Although if is difficult to assign a monetary value to an intangible, it is not impossible to estimate an intangible's impact.[2]

Consider first the tangibles. An organization that has taken steps to reduce wastewater discharges to its sanitary sewer and, thus, to the wastewater treatment plant will pay less for wastewater treatment. It may further be able to recycle and reuse what was previously a waste. If the organization had to purchase capacity from the wastewater treatment plant, it could sell back the unused portion.

Now let us look at the intangibles that generally do not appear on the budget and may be considered more as externalities, i.e., they benefit

---

[2] Note: It is recognized formal quantification of satisfaction can be done via Likert scale, though the process can be cumbersome. Consequently, an organization's empirical evidence of satisfaction can suffice as reasonable input for evaluation.

society as opposed to the organization. By reducing its loading on the wastewater treatment plant, the treatment plant may be able to delay or eliminate expansion of capital equipment and associated operating expenses. Potentially it can hold rates down for the general public and other organizations because they don't have to compensate for the capital expansion and expenses.

In the end, however, this can translate into an improved public perception of that organization for taking steps to reduce its impact on the environment; thus, further increasing sales because the organization is more environmentally and socially responsible than its competitors.

Direct and Indirect Costs and Benefits

Direct costs are those expenditures borne directly by the organization. They are represented by items such as salaries, energy costs, construction, capital, raw materials, disposal and treatment of waste, taxes, fees, and insurance associated with running the organization. Generally, direct costs are planned and typically appear as budget items.

Indirect costs are those expenses incurred by the organizations that result from sources outside the organization. They are usually unplanned and, therefore, not budget items, but must still be borne by the organization. Indirect costs include fines and penalties, cleanup, litigation, settlements, or any other unexpected or unforeseen cost. It is often the case that most organizations do not evaluate the potential cost of their actions to this level of detail. Thus, it is particularly important for organizations to avoid indirect costs in order to dispel the uncertainty associated with them. Nonetheless, it is equally important that organizations understand and consider both direct and potential indirect costs during the decision making process.

Indirect costs are often the result of society's attempt to internalize externalities generated by an organization. There are, however, ways to force the polluter to pay via regulatory means. Under such programs, some external costs may manifest themselves in such a way as to convert them into internal costs that are borne by the organization. Those costs may come in the form of increased insurance premiums. They can also produce higher bank interest rates due to increased risk, adverse effects on public health and safety that manifest themselves in increased cost for protective services (e.g., fire department and hazardous material response crews), and negative consumer perception that impact purchases.

The question then comes up as to the relevancy of defining external costs as truly direct costs. If the organization does not improve or remove its external liabilities, which under the "polluter pays" precept will become internalized, it runs the risk of failing to compete with similar firms. Once costs move from the external to the internal realm they begin to affect the ability of the organization to compete.

Why should an organization care about externalities? There are a number of speculative variables that can come into focus that can be difficult to quantify, but can help an organization see how external variables can quickly translate into internal issues. Examples of those variables include negative perceptions and possible legal action against the organization by neighbors and the public in general, boycotts of the organization and its products, increased agency inspection brought about by public complaints, and chastisement by industry associations for failure to act as a responsible organization.

Involvement at All Levels of the Organization

Environmental costs and economics as they relate to the organization are, in many cases, driven by the way in which it manages its environmental issues. While it must be acknowledged that regulations play a significant role in the costs an organization has to pay in order to comply with them, it is ultimately the organization's decision of what it will manufacture and sell that determines what regulations will apply to them. It becomes a corporate strategic decision on how to best mitigate the environmental impacts through its environmental management program.

An organization's successful environmental management program recognizes that environmental issues are also safety issues. For instance, the environmental consequences of disposal of hazardous waste material in an unsafe manner that causes pollution of the air, water, and land, and safety threats not only to the workers, but also the population in general. Safety has improved the profitability of organizations by keeping employees free from harm and by reducing losses of material assets and associated insurance costs.

With many competing initiatives faced by organizations today, why would an organization spend more now on environmental concerns than is legally required, especially when organizations want to operate lean in order to be as competitive as possible?

If technology, products, processes, and customer needs were all fixed, then the conclusion that regulation must raise costs would be inevitable. But organizations operate in the real world of dynamic competition, not in the static world. They are constantly finding innovative solutions to pressure of all sorts – from competitors, customers, and regulators.

Properly designed environmental standards can trigger innovations that lower total cost of a product and improve its value. Such innovations allow organizations to use a range of inputs more productively – from raw materials to energy to labor – thus offsetting the costs of improving environmental impact and ending the stalemate. Ultimately, this enhanced resource productivity makes organizations more competitive, not less.

Policy makers, business leaders, and environmentalists have focused on the static cost impacts of environmental regulation and have ignored the more important offsetting productivity benefits from innovation. Regulators tend to set regulations in ways that deter innovation. Organizations, in turn, oppose and delay regulations instead of innovating to address them.

In order to deploy a change in environmental behavior within the organization, it is necessary to change the mindset of the organization's management hierarchy. An effective environmental management program requires support at all levels within the organization. This means making available the necessary tool to implement change via funding, management support, and deploying the tools presented in this book to substantiate the benefits of deploying a given environmental activity, or group of activities.

Calculating Net Present Value

Do not let the formula scare you—it is a simple way to calculate if there is a net benefit by using the following equation:

$$NPV = \sum_{n=0}^{t} \frac{(B_t - C_t)}{(1+d)^t},$$

where NPV is net present value, B_t and C_t are benefit and cost at a specific time, and t and d are the life of the activity and discount rate, respectively. The discount rate is based upon the interest rate that the organization can reasonably expect to earn if it invested the money as opposed to doing the activity.

Net present value compares the value of a dollar in present terms versus what it would be worth in the future if it had been invested at the discount rate. NPV assumes that by taking into account that discount rate over that same period of time that there may or may not be a reason to pursue the activity. In other words, it would be more advisable to invest the money as opposed to doing the project. If the NPV is a positive number, then there is an indication that the activity should be done, but it may not be a compelling reason. The analyst needs to determine if the NPV is positive enough to pursue and that can only be assessed by each individual organization or department. The organization needs to decide on an appropriate discount rate, although 5% is generally acceptable.

Table 1 presents attributes, their description, and how they can be measured. This list is by no means all-inclusive, and each organization is unique. Therefore, the analyst will need to decide, based on their unique situation, which attributes to include or omit from their calculus.

Table 1. Benefit-Cost Attributes, Descriptions, and Operational Measures.

Attribute	Description	Operational Measure
Sale / lease / cost of proprietary environmental technology	Cost to develop proprietary pollution control equipment that is designed and engineered by the organization. Ownership rights allow the firm to license, sell, or lease the technology or construction rights to other firms.	Measured directly by purchase and sale invoices. Purchase invoices include the following costs: administrative, design, engineering, materials, and construction labor. Sale invoices include: revenues from licensing, sale, or lease options to other firms.
Organization's reputation among business consumers	Consumers' willingness to purchase organization's products driven by environmental performance. Consumers will preferentially align themselves with organizations whose environmental performance will not lead to interruptions of product supply.	Measured directly by sales figures. This variable may be subjective because there may be other variables influencing the outcome in addition to environmental impacts.
Productivity of employees; reduction in employee injuries and illnesses	Employee safety encompasses injury and illness rates. Improvements in environmental issues can yield dramatic reduction in injuries and illnesses.	Measured directly by illness and injury incidence rate. Results may need to be modified to account for issues other than environmental, including changes to the safety program and incidences related to personal behavior,

Attribute	Description	Operational Measure
Productivity of employees; reduction in employee injuries and illnesses (continued)	Examples include: noise (hearing), dust control (respiratory), vapors and fumes (numerous health impacts like headaches, nausea, and cancer). Organizations that operate in an environmentally conscientious manner will likely have more productive employees (e.g., fewer employees to do more work) and be able to offer better wage rates.	like smoking, diet, and exercise. Employee productivity can be measured by comparing production versus employee enrollment and correlated with changes in the environmental management program. Wage rates may be compared with other similarly sized organizations.
Productivity enhancements / reaction completion / product yield / product quality	This attribute measures the input versus the output, specifically, the impact of environmental improvements on any increase in productivity enhancements, chemical reaction completion, and product yield. Productivity enhancements refer to items such as faster process rates, purer products, and new or	Productivity enhancements may be measured directly from production volumes, analysis of product purity, and product performance compared to previous versions. Reaction completion may be measured directly and evaluated for desirable and useful constituents. Side reactions do not automatically imply undesirable reactions as there may be opportunities for these new products in the marketplace. Product yield measure directly by ratio of desired output versus raw material input. Energy and

Table 1. Benefit-Cost Attributes, Descriptions, and Operational Measures.

(continued)

Attribute	Description	Operational Measure
Productivity enhancements / reaction completion / product yield / product quality (continued)	improved product lines. Reaction completion refers to optimized chemical reactions that do not produce excess undesirable constituents. Product yield is the amount of desired product synthesized. Conscientious environmental behavior and less waste leads to energy and water conservation, thus cutting costs. Production of less waste initiates fewer process upsets and greater process reliability and efficiency. Off quality material that must be recycled or scrapped adversely impacts product quality and output.	water costs measure directly from utility bills. Production reliability measure and statistically correlated with changes in environmental behavior, like energy and water conservation programs. Reliability is the percentage calculated from the number of hours the process operated (O_A) versus the number of hours it could have operated (O_P), or $$\text{Re}\,liability = \frac{O_A}{O_P} \times 100\%.$$ Other contributing factors must be taken into account and deducted from the potential output volume, such as mechanical downtime, power outages, work stoppage, etc.
Pre-consumer recycling	Recycling refers to product that may be degraded, but that can be returned to the process and always remained associated with the process. An	Recycling measured directly from production logs that should track how much material is being returned to the process. Raw material replacement may be calculated directly by

Table 1. Benefit-Cost Attributes, Descriptions, and Operational Measures.
(continued)

Attribute	Description	Operational Measure
Pre-consumer recycling (continued)	example of this is the steel mill that trims sheet metal and returns the trimmings directly back into the process. Raw material usage increase to make up for incomplete or wasteful activities. If there is waste, then the raw material is not being utilized to its fullest potential; thus, raw material usage increase in an amount equal to the amount needed to replace the waste.	determining the amount of the specific raw material treated, discharged, emitted, and disposed. The value of additional raw material to make up for waste may be calculated by multiplying the total waste of the raw material by its value as a raw material
Investor perceptions	If an organization enjoys good environmental performance, then investors should be more likely to invest in the firm. The difficulty in measuring this arises because there are competing reasons to invest. For example, the investor may like the product line and diversity, the organization's sales are strong, or the	Measured directly from discrete investments, stock market, and bond ratings. Small organizations should be able to obtain a fairly accurate figure because investors can invest directly in the firm without necessarily investing by the stock market. Investor in small firms can be questioned directly regarding how much of their investment is due to environmental performance. The stock market can be used to measure investor perceptions of large organizations. It is

Table 1. Benefit-Cost Attributes, Descriptions, and Operational Measures.
(continued)

Attribute	Description	Operational Measure
Investor perceptions (continued)	product is innovative and lacks competition in the marketplace. It may be quite difficult to separate the environmental component from these other variables.	much more difficult to quantify how much of their investment is driven by environmental performance.
Compliance (staff, legal, paperwork)	This is the cost to retain legal representation, administration and secretarial staff, and documentation to satisfy regulatory compliance. Generally, more complex and recurrent compliance issues require more attention, time, and follow up.	Measured directly by distributing costs associated with environmental activities.
Regulatory agency relationships	If the relationship between the regulatory agency and the organization is adversarial, then there may be less likelihood of a partnership being developed. Furthermore, it may drive the agency to be more active in its oversight of the firm. The agency relationship may	Subjective measure. May be difficult to quantify other than as a positive, negative, or neutral impact. The organization should be fully cognizant of its relationship with the agencies and, at the very least, be able to rate its standing with them. The organization should be aware that as inspection frequency increases there is a greater chance that something will be found out of compliance.

Table 1. Benefit-Cost Attributes, Descriptions, and Operational Measures.
(continued)

Attribute	Description	Operational Measure
Regulatory agency relationships (continued)	influence how quickly it processes permits for process expansion or modification at the organization. The number of enforcement actions taken by the regulatory agencies can lead to increased fines and penalties, curtailment or cessation of operations, and civil or criminal action. The number of enforcement actions tends to mean external (i.e., agency) help and oversight that most companies do not want.	Repetitive enforcement activity will increase penalties exponentially. Furthermore, in cases where agencies integrate information among one another, enforcement activity by one agency may drive another agency to look more closely at what the firm is doing related to that agency's rules and regulations.
Insurance costs	Protection against environmental liability and damages. Firms that carry excess environmental liability will likely be subject to higher insurance costs in order to protect the insurer.	Measured directly by change in insurance costs as a result of environmental behavior. This figure can be influenced by regulatory actions or settlements against the organization.
Interest rates	The interest rate at which the organization is charged by financial	Measured directly. Information regarding changes in loan rate should be available from the financial

Table 1. Benefit-Cost Attributes, Descriptions, and Operational Measures.
(continued)

Attribute	Description	Operational Measure
Interest rates (continued)	institutions to borrow money to expand, modify, or improve their operations. Like insurance costs, organizations that carry excess environmental liability will likely be subject to higher loan rates in order to protect the lending institution.	institution. For example, the financial institution should be able to address whether or not an increase in loan rate is the result of environmental issues.
Equipment (control technology)	This is different than sale/lease/cost of environmental technology. It refers to purchased equipment for the purpose of pollution abatement.	Measured directly from purchase invoices. Costs should include not only the capital, but also any other expenses like energy, water, personnel, and construction.
Cleanup	This attribute includes on-site cleanup of spills and leaks, and off-site remedial actions like Superfund.	Measured directly from service and purchase invoices.
Fines and penalties	Fines represent a firmly established amount that the organization must pay for an infraction of the regulations, or due to exceeding a permit limit. Penalties are charges over and	Measured directly from letters generated by the regulatory agency specifying the amount of the fine and penalty.

Table 1. Benefit-Cost Attributes, Descriptions, and Operational Measures.
(continued)

Attribute	Description	Operational Measure
Fines and penalties (continued)	above the fine and may be prorated based on the amount the firm exceeds the acceptable limit.	
Permits, fees, and taxes	This attribute is the initial cost to prepare a permit. It includes fees paid to regulatory agencies to process and issue the permit, and any costs incurred by the organization to prepare the application. Also included are fees to renew permits, hazardous waste taxes, and registration fees for EPA and state waste disposal numbers.	Measured directly from invoices from federal, state, county, and local regulatory agencies, and from distributed costs for the organization's employees to prepare the applications.
Monitoring frequency	This attribute refers to monitoring that the organization does, or needs to do, in order to assure that it operates in compliance. Monitoring includes: wastewater sampling, annual emission source tests, continual emissions monitoring, and hazardous waste inspections.	Measured directly from invoices from laboratory invoices, distributed personnel costs, and emissions testing contractor bills.

Table 1. Benefit-Cost Attributes, Descriptions, and Operational Measures.
(continued)

Attribute	Description	Operational Measure
Treatment and disposal of waste; emission credits and costs / discharge credits and costs	In many cases, before waste can be disposed of, it must undergo specific treatment options. This includes neutralization, stabilization, incineration, immobilization, etc. Ultimately, it includes disposal costs. Attributes in this category also include the cost to treat wastewater at a wastewater treatment facility and the cost of air emissions. Air regulations require organizations in non-attainment areas for priority pollutants (NO_X, SO_X, CO, PM, ozone [from volatile organic compounds—VOCs], and lead)[3] to purchase emission reduction credits for the right to pollute if they modify existing, or install new sources of, emissions. By the	This attribute is measured directly from bills received from treatment and disposal facilities, or, in the case of on-site treatment, from invoices for the materials and distributed costs for personnel resources used to treat the waste. Wastewater and air emission bills submitted by each respective agency, city, or county can be used as operational measures. Emission reduction credit value is negotiated between the buyer and seller organizations; their value is determined directly from sale or purchase invoices.

---

[3] NO_X are oxides of nitrogen, SO_X are oxides of sulfur, CO is carbon monoxide, PM is particulate matter.

Table 1. Benefit-Cost Attributes, Descriptions, and Operational Measures.
(continued)

Attribute	Description	Operational Measure
Treatment and disposal of waste; emission credits and costs / discharge credits and costs (continued)	same token, if the firm reduces its emissions it can bank the emission credits for use later, or sell, lease, or trade them.	

How to do it

Let us assume for the sake of example that we have an organization that manufactures computer circuit boards. That form applies the Refined Benefit-Cost Model in its decision making process when deciding if it should proceed with an environmental activity. That activity, or group of activities, could mean that they decide to pursue a certain behavior like a new environmental program or to initiate a capital project.

Step One

Collect information based on past expenditures or estimate them related to the best available information.

Step Two

Using the criteria of Table 1 we can insert the measured or estimated amounts collected in Step One and apply the data to each attribute, where applicable, into Table 2. This example will look at how pursuing an activity pays out over a five year period of time. In this example we are recovering the solvent, tetrachloroethylene, and recycling, reusing, and selling it. Concurrently, the organization in question maintains a robust environmental management program and all the benefits derived from doing so.

Table 2. Refined Benefit-Cost Attributes and Descriptions for Hypothetical Organization.

No.	Attribute	Description
1	Sale / lease/ cost of proprietary environmental technology	The organization has sold the design, which cost $85,000 to develop during year two, to a pollution control firm for residuals (10% of the value of each sale). There have been three units sold during each of the last two years, with the trend expected to continue, at a sale value of $150,000 per unit. The organization's residuals for the sale of the three units are worth $45,000 annually.
2	Organization's reputation among business consumers	Positive consumer perception has kept sales strong, with an increase of about one percent per year for the last five years. Base year sales (i.e., five years ago) were $30 million per year. Annual contribution of growth from consumer perceptions breaks down as follows: (1) $300,000, (2) $303,000, (3) $306,030, (4) $309,090, and (5) $312,181, or $1,530,302 over five years.
3	Productivity of employees; reduction in employee injuries and illnesses	The organization has incurred no additional costs for inspection, monitoring, or enforcement. It enjoys a good relationship with the community with no outstanding public safety or health issues. Since the organization implements it environmental management program, it saves $30,000 annually in health insurance premiums, employee lost time, and medical treatment costs. The organization has been able to entice quality management personnel and technicians. Its employees are enjoying the highest wages in the organizational sector. They are inclined to remain with the organization and perform well for it. Employees enjoy their working

Table 2. Refined Benefit-Cost Attributes and Descriptions for Hypothetical Organization.
(continued)

No.	Attribute	Description
	Productivity of employees; reduction in employee injuries and illnesses (continued)	conditions and make a lifetime career out of it. Because employees stay, the organization saves $15,000 per year in training costs that would otherwise be needed for employee turnover.
4	Productivity enhancements / reaction completion / product yield / product quality	During the base year (i.e., five years ago) the organization operated at 80 percent efficiency, or 600,000 units per year, assuming that 100 percent efficiency is equal to 750,000 units per year, with a sale value of $50 per unit. Due to the fact that its environmental quality is in a continuous improvement mode, the firm has been able to concentrate on product quality and productivity enhancements. It operates at 88 percent efficiency, or 660,000 units annually. Its product yield has improved by 60,000 units over base year production. This has contributed to an increase of $3.0 million per year in sales revenues. Energy costs have decreased per unit of production due to less waste, higher operating efficiency, and improved quality with fewer defects. The organization saves $100,000 annually due to reduced energy costs. In order to reduce waste, the organization has improved quality driving it to reduce rework. As a result, production value has increased by 0.5 percent on a basis of $33 million (i.e., 660,000 units x $50 per unit) annually, or $165,000 per year.
5	Pre-consumer recycling	The organization uses virgin tetrachloroethylene to clean its circuit boards. Once the tetrachloroethylene

No.	Attribute	Description
	Recycling (continued)	becomes contaminated the organization uses it in its machine parts washers and sells some to a garage in the community to use to clean automobile engines and parts. Virgin tetrachloroethylene has a value of $85 per liter. The organization uses 6,000 liters per year at an annual cost of $510,000. It does not need to purchase additional solvent for its parts washers. It sells what it does not use in its parts washers (2,500 liters per year) to a local garage. The garage saves a considerable amount of money by not buying virgin tetrachloroethylene because it does not need virgin tetrachloroethylene to clean automobile parts. The garage pays the organization $2 per liter per year, for an annual revenue of $5,000. It settles mercury and collects 75 kilograms per year, which it sells to a recycling firm for $95 per kilogram, or $7,125 annually.
6	Investor perceptions	Investor confidence is high because the organization is showing strong growth and because there are no environmental compliance issues. Stock value has grown $5 per share per year. There are 300,000 shares. This means a growth in investor perception of $1.5 million annually.
7	Compliance (staff, legal, paperwork)	There have been no compliance issues. Although compliance paperwork has been reduced, the organization continues to manage environmental programs to a high level of control; therefore, there is no net change in its compliance costs.
8	Regulatory agency relationships	Due to its excellent environmental behavior, the organization enjoys a

Table 2. Refined Benefit-Cost Attributes and Descriptions for Hypothetical Organization.
(continued)

No.	Attribute	Description
	Regulatory agency relationships (continued)	positive environmental relationship. The organization has been registered as an ISO 14001 entity; so, regulatory agency inspection frequency has been reduced to once per year for hazardous waste, air quality, and water quality. Due to its superlative record, there have been no enforcement actions.
9	Insurance costs	Risk insurance premiums have dropped by $25,000 per year because of the organization's continued good performance.
10	Interest rates	The organization enjoys premium interest rates on loans. The organization is taking a loan of $5 million to make capital improvements. The best loan rate it can find is six percent per annum. Assume a complete pay back of the next five years at $1 million per year plus interest. Interest per annum breaks down as follows: (1) $300,000, (2) $240,000, (3) $180,000, (4) $120,000, and (5) $60,000, for a total of $900,000 for five years.
11	Equipment (control technology)	The organization has developed and uses a vapor and liquid collection and control system that nets almost complete recovery of tetrachloroethylene. The firm spent $40,000 to design, construct, and install it during year zero (i.e., pre-startup). Based on full recovery of solvent, the organization avoids purchasing solvent for its parts washers, where it used 1,000 liters annually, and sells the remainder to a local garage.
12	Cleanup	Due to the careful control of its chemicals and wastes, there are no cleanup costs.

**Table 2. Refined Benefit-Cost Attributes and Descriptions for
Hypothetical Organization.**
(continued)

13	Fines and penalties	There have been no fines or penalties.
14	Permits, fees, and taxes	The air permit for the solvent recovery system cost $880. The organization's annual waste fees have dropped by $5,000 per year.
15	Monitoring frequency	This attribute refers to monitoring that the organization does, or needs to do, in order to assure that it operates in compliance. Monitoring includes: wastewater sampling, annual emission source tests, continual emissions monitoring, and hazardous waste inspections.
16	Treatment and disposal of waste; emission credits and costs / discharge credits and costs	In many cases, before waste can be disposed of, it must undergo specific treatment options. This includes neutralization, stabilization, incineration, immobilization, etc. Ultimately, it includes disposal costs. Attributes in this category also include the cost to treat wastewater at a wastewater treatment facility and the cost of air emissions. Air regulations require organizations in non-attainment areas for priority pollutants (NO_X, SO_X, CO, PM, ozone [from VOCs], and lead) to purchase emission reduction credits for the right to pollute if they modify existing, or install new sources of emissions. By the same token, if the firm reduces its emissions it can bank the emission credits for use later, or sell, lease, or trade them. This example assumes that the organization sells excess emission reduction credits to other organizations for $37,000 during year three and $5,000 during year four.

Step Three

Insert the figures assigned to each variable into Table 3. This step assigns benefits and costs to each attribute.

Table 2. Refined Benefit-Cost Matrix.

No.	Attribute	Benefit ($/year)	Cost ($/year)
1	Sale / lease / cost of proprietary environmental technology	45,000	Yr 2: 85,000
2	Organization's reputation among business consumers	Yr 1: 300,000 Yr 2: 303,000 Yr 3: 306,030 Yr 4: 309,090 Yr 5: 312,181 Total: 1,530,302	
3	Productivity of employees; reduction in employee injuries	15,000 30,000	
4	Productivity enhancements / reaction completion / product yield / product quality	3,000,000 100,000 165,000	
5	Pre-consumer recycling	7,125 5,000	510,000
6	Investor perceptions	1,500,000	
7	Compliance (staff, paperwork, legal)		0
8	Regulatory agency relationships		0
9	Insurance costs	25,000	
10	Interest rates		Yr 1: 300,000 Yr 2: 240,000 Yr 3: 180,000 Yr 4: 120,000 Yr 5: 60,000 Total: 900,000

Table 2. Refined Benefit-Cost Matrix.
(continued)

11	Equipment (control technology)		Yr 0 (i.e., pre-startup): 40,000
12	Cleanup		0
13	Fines and penalties		0
14	Permits, fees, and taxes	5,000	Yr 0: 880
15	Monitoring frequency	Yr 3: 6,525 Yr 4: 6,525 Yr 5: 6,525 Total: 19,575	
16	Treatment and disposal of waste	Yr 3: 37,000 Yr 4: 5,000 Total: 42,000	
	Five-year Total	26,077,501	3,450,880

Step Four

Input the information into Table 3 which includes expenditures, costs, and benefits during the five-year life of the activity analyzed using a discount rate of seven percent and a government tax rate on capital at 35 percent. While the 35-percent tax is generally applicable to capital costs, it has been applied to the total in order to be more conservative. Parenthetical values in Tables 3 and 4 indicate costs.

Table 3. Net Present Value.
(Cost and Savings Assumptions $ in thousands)

	Year 0	Year 1	Year 2	Year 3	Year 4	Year 5
Capital Costs	(45)		(85)			
Operating Costs						
Pre-consumer recycling		(510)	(510)	(510)	(510)	(510)
Interest payments		(300)	(240)	(180)	(120)	(60)

Table 3. Net Present Value.
(Cost and Savings Assumptions $ in thousands)
(continued)

	Year 0	Year 1	Year 2	Year 3	Year 4	Year 5
Permit	(1)					
Total Operating Costs	(1)	(810)	(750)	(690)	(630)	(570)
Benefits						
Sale of proprietary environmental technology		45	45	45	45	45
Organization's reputation among business consumers		300	303	306	309	312
Employee productivity		15	15	15	15	15
Reduction in employee injuries and health costs		30	30	30	30	30
Product yield		3,000	3,000	3,000	3,000	3,000
Productivity enhancements		100	100	100	100	100
Product quality		165	165	165	165	165
Pre-consumer recycling (sale of excess to recycling firm)		7	7	7	7	7
Pre-consumer recycling (sale of excess to local garage)		5	5	5	5	5

Table 3. Net Present Value.
(Cost and Savings Assumptions $ in thousands)
(continued)

	Year 0	Year 1	Year 2	Year 3	Year 4	Year 5
Investor perceptions		1,500	1,500	1,500	1,500	1,500
Insurance savings		25	25	25	25	25
Permits, fees, and taxes		5	5	5	5	5
Monitoring frequency				7	7	7
Emission credits				37	5	
Total Benefits		5,197	5,200	5,247	5,218	5,216

Table 4 presents time distributed cost and benefit details during that same five-year period. Here the values have been transferred from Table 3 and placed in their respective year. Year 0 represents preparations that take place during pre-startup activity. *Total cash before tax* is the sum of the capital, benefits, and costs. *Total cash after tax* is the total cash before tax times the government tax rate. For this example we are using 35 percent. So $1.00 - 0.35 = 0.65$, which is our multiplier to obtain *total cash after tax* (e.g., for Year 1: $4,387 x 0.65 = $2,852). *Tax depreciation* is determined by straight line depreciation in the example. *Net cash after tax* is *total cash after tax* + tax *depreciation help*. Finally, *cumulative after tax payout* is calculated by adding each year's *net cash after tax* to each preceding year's *cumulative after tax payout*.

Table 4. Net Present Value Details.
($ in thousands)

	Year 0	Year 1	Year 2	Year 3	Year 4	Year 5
Capital						
Control technology	(40)		(85)			
Benefits						
Total		5,197	5,200	5,247	5,218	5,216
Costs						
Operating costs	(1)	(810)	(750)	(690)	(630)	(570)
Total cash before tax	(41)	4,387	4,365	4,557	4,588	4,646
Total cash after tax	(41)	2,852	2,837	2,962	2,982	3,020
Tax depreciation help		8	8	36	36	36
Net cash after tax	(41)	2,860	2,845	2,998	3,018	3,056
Cumulative after tax payout	(41)	2,819	5,664	8,662	11,680	14,736

Step 5

Now substitute the cumulative after tax payout (which accounts for all benefits and costs at the 35-percent tax rate) for the five-year period into the NPV equation along with the discount rate and time period as follows:

$$NPV = \sum_{n=0}^{5} \frac{14,736}{(1+0.07)^5},$$

$$= \frac{14,736}{(1.07)^5},$$

$$= \frac{14,649}{1.40},$$

$$= 10,506.$$

This translates to a net present value (NPV) after five years of $10,506,000. By this example it has been demonstrated that an organization's active environmental management approach has been worth the investment in time, energy, and money. Its investment in emission controls and the strengthening of its overall environment management program have paid out with significant dividends. With a net present value after five years of $10.5 million, it is hard to argue against its investment in environmental management.

The majority of benefits come from productivity enhancement through improved process reliability. As the organization produces less waste, more marketable product goes out the door and into the hands of consumers. It is easy to see the advantages as the organization produces less waste, how it can be translated into other segments of the organization. Reductions in waste lead to lower disposal costs, more recycle and lower raw material replacement costs. Also, reduced waste means that there should be an attendant increase in product yield. This is especially true with organizations that engage in chemical manufacturing operations.

Investor perception, another key factor in this example, may be driven by the results of productivity enhancements. Also, investors are more likely to invest in organizations that do not have the risk of shutting down or long term liabilities that may be associated with organizations that do not have an environmental conscience. Although there are many variables that determine where an investor will put his money, more and more organizations, like financial institutions and insurance companies, are being influenced by an organization's environmental performance. They, too, want a high degree of certainty that their investments will be safe.

While it can be argued that the costs and benefits presented in this example have been grossly underestimated and overestimated, respectively, the main point of this exercise is twofold. First, it is a demonstration of the technique used to perform a benefit-cost analysis. It shows the level of detail in which anyone needs to engage in order to portray accurately whether or not an activity, program, or project should be pursued.

Second, it demonstrates how careful analysis can point to problems within an organization and provide an impetus to take corrective action without being driven to do so by regulations. Many of the costs are related to waste or poor environmental management methods that are not necessarily connected to regulatory controls or costs. Because organizations have the potential to accomplish so much outside the regulatory arena to cut their losses (e.g., reducing generated waste, source reduction, employee training, chemical substitution, and enhanced product quality), they do not need permission to do so. It makes good economic sense to initiate programs that reduce losses and waste because it feeds back into so much of the rest of the business.

48

Global Warming / Global Climate Change

The purpose of this chapter is not to enter the debate about global warming or global climate change. It is meant to convey the message that any decision requires that the solution to the problem not only implies an environmental benefit, but also does so in an economically efficient manner.

Whether one subscribes to a global warming or global climate change philosophy, the debate will continue—but this is not the venue for repudiating any particular slant but rather a self-help guide to making sound choices. Regardless of what drives one to implement environmentally responsible decisions, it makes intuitive sense that all of us will benefit if we are good stewards of Planet Earth's resources.

It would be a travesty to spend trillions of dollars globally to control something which may be driven more by naturally-occurring events and random cycles as opposed to man's direct impact. At this point it would be speculative, at best, to assume that one side of the debate is exactly right in its interpretation of cause and effect.

The real point here would be to answer the following non-exclusive questions from both an environmental benefit and economic benefit standpoint: (1) Should anything be done to mitigate the effects of climate change? (2) If anything should be done, then to what extent? (3) Based on whatever is done, will the associated effect warrant the expenditure?

Obviously, if it makes sense to control greenhouse gases from an economic standpoint, then the organization should do it regardless of government intervention. The best way to determine what, if anything, should be done is to use the tools provided in this book to support and validate the decision-making process. This includes doing everything possible, doing something, or doing nothing to mitigate the event.

The techniques presented in this book are not limited solely to environmental issues. They are applicable to any situation where an expenditure must be made. It is true for any activity an organization plans to pursue, not just environmental. It includes decisions to expand operations, to change formulations, to spend more on marketing, and so on. These decisions must not be made in a vacuum. Applying benefit-cost analysis of the activity will provide insight as to the efficacy of proceeding with it and the potential benefits and risks.

Even the lay person can benefit from this approach. For example, if a homeowner is trying to decide if he / she should remodel their home, then he / she should use these techniques to decide if there will be a return on investment or if it is worth the expenditure merely for their enjoyment. It can also provide direction as to what specific improvements will lead to the biggest return on investment at the lowest risk. These techniques provide users with a rational, quantitative approach to aid them in making choices among activities and delineating within them what should or should not be pursued.

Reference List

Randall, Robert E., June 1999, Refined Benefit-Cost Analysis of Federal
    Environmental Regulations & Corporate Strategic Planning: A
    Case Study of the Procter & Gamble Company, PhD
    Dissertation.

Index

www.ingramcontent.com/pod-product-compliance
Lightning Source LLC
Chambersburg PA
CBHW021916190326
41519CB00008B/798